In the Shadow Country

Elena Cisneros

TAVERN BOOKS

PORTLAND

ISBN-13: 978-1-935635-87-1 (paperback)
ISBN-13: 978-1-935635-88-8 (hardcover)

LCCN: 2019931274

FIRST EDITION

98765432 First Printing

TAVERN BOOKS
Union Station
800 NW 6th Avenue #255
Portland, Oregon 97209
www.tavernbooks.org

Table of Contents

I

II

III

I.

In the Shadow Country

I am the poet who dreams
Of ships, eagles and smoke.
I see the dead get up in the morning,
Sit on the porch and scare the dogs.
I know the words to the rhythm song;
It kills children, blinds cats.
I hum it in this cold room.
I know the words to the prayer
For the goldfish, sunfish and mountain flower.
I write it in the tree with blood.
I see the shadow of the hanged daughter
Against the wall.
I hear the women moan at the gravesite.
I hear the ticks of silver as the men load the bullets
In the old guns.
I hear the hooves of horses on the wet ground.
I see them painted and unreal with spirits riding
On their backs.
I buried enough I don't want to anymore.
I take the black knife, put it to my wrist,
Only to stab the wall over and over and over.
I see the ghost walk down the stairs
Into the cold dark basement.

I watch the boy follow it.
What does he see?
I trace the bullet holes in the wall,
Drive past the burned out houses and trailers.
I know my homeland is prisoner of war camp #334.
I know at night spirits walk down from the mass grave at Wounded Knee,
They look around. I wonder,
What do they see?
I take the dead fawn, bring it back to life
With lamplight and well water.
I take the wild roses, paint them with resin
From the pipe.
They have grown in abundance, tingle my fingertips.
I drive cars off cliffs
Only to exit through the radio
And burst into lilacs.
I am silenced by the phone ringing in the night,
The moon in summer
And the red star in the morning.
I see the road get smaller,
The flags get older and the tobacco turn to dust.
Somewhere an eagle is a man, who prefers to sit in the tree,
Look to the night sky and count stars.
All the animals come out from the dark
And marvel at the miracle.
I hear people talk about death.

It comes smiling, leaves them screaming,
It comes into the rooms of children,
The beds of women, the cars of men.
I hear people talk of a tall man walking the hills.
The dogs howl as he passes in long heavy strides
Across the plains.
I hear of a shadow hand that clutches warm hearts
And strips them bare in the moonlight.

The Unity of Objects

Wrap them in fine silk and bring them to me. Bring me light. Bring me dark. Bring me the silence of a pale morning. Bring me the fear of a blood sunrise. Bring me the dust of small dark places. Bring me the ice of frozen flowers. Bring me the branches of a lone pine. Bring me the bright paint and pour it on the feathers of the owl. Bring pictures of abandoned houses in dark forests where the trees are so dead they no longer bloom. Bring me the bodies of mine canaries. Bring me old 45s and the strings of banjos. Bring me the guitar picks and fingertips of delta blues musicians. Bring me blades of grass. Bring me fireflies and butterflies and the legs of centipedes. Bring the quiet. Bring the silence after. Bring the spear of a lost tribe. Bring me their names.

Traces

Tracing the world in streaked small lines on the inside of the car's rear
    window—
My body pitched into the crawlspace of this rear window—
My stomach empty but for the cereal and water—
Dreaming with eyes open to the tune of country honk—
Steel guitars and dirty violins pumping in my ribcage—
Open sky at my fingertips—
The sunset does not bleed but blankets my body in color—
The turn of the radio dial and I am again—
Tracing the world on the inside of this car's rear window—
The face of my mother illuminated by light from the radio dial—

Shame

I go past the truck
With the two boys sitting
In the faded bucket seats.
I see ahead of me
A small black horse.
"I know you," it says;
"We used to be friends."
I can't remember the horse's name.
I try and hold my gaze elsewhere.
The horse is skinny, patchy and sweating.
I drive past, my stomach buzzing
With nerves.
I am not skinny, patchy, and my car
Has the air conditioner on.
The black horse follows, running along
The side of the road.

I Step out and Into

Carrying my lamp
I step out and into
The black bowl of night.

There is no sound,
Not my breath,
Not my heart,
Not my footsteps.

I see their eyes.

I see them waiting
In the thick brush.
One moves ahead
And there is no sound.

We wait together for my move.

On the Hill

The smell of cedar, sage and blood
Overcomes me.
The tree, before it a man and horse
Both steady and humble.

I feel protected.
I could walk this whole country and never find it
But here, on the hill.

The Moth

When I feel like being holy
I place a warm light
Behind its frail body.
Cast its shadow
On my face.

Saint Francis, South Dakota

It's summer on 1070.

All the shadows come and lay their heads on the tops of houses.

This is how we live; doors open, pups on the front steps, our mothers
      cooking dinner

And the graveyard full of trees.

Nothing Shall Touch Them

Jesus came from the desert on bare feet.

He found the Baptist alone by the water carving a ship.

The Baptist stood, put the ship on sand, and led Jesus to the water.

Underneath the golden sky the Baptist cleaned the smell of death from
      the son.

The Baptist spoke not a word as Jesus walked away. The Baptist went
      back to his ship.

Inside all the little people slept. The Baptist placed the ship on the water.

Somewhere a child is singing and the people wake.

Directions to a Grieving Ghost

Drive to the badlands
Turn the headlights off
Remember your uncle
A green falling star
Realize everyone will die
Be alright with it

Brother Was Tired

Brother was tired
Any other day brother was clean and smiling
Always had a joke to tell

Brother was a chemical reaction

He askcd for money
Brother had to go somewhere after he had been nowhere for hours
He had to go where there were streetlights, all-night gas stations and
         fast food

Brother was gray in the doorway

Nights like this were tricky
Nights like this people left and never came back
Nights like this people became stories
Nights like this bad dreams ruled the world

A voice came
Brother
The news came
A car wreck
So began the story

Brother hit black ice
Crawled out of the wreck and ran into the hills
Twenty below
Brother's lungs froze

He told the story again and again
Mother listened
Mother got the coffee on
So began the ritual

I Remember the Night My Mother Disappeared

That big Buick
Flying down a lonely road in the Montana night
She was arguing with him
I sat up to see her face
Then she was gone
A cold wind of blackness choked me
When she opened the car door
The Buick kept flying
Down a lonely road in the Montana night

Searching Blue for Black

I am the bird in the tree. The lone blackbird in the tree.
The one with the broken wing. The one with the darting head
Upwards, searching blue for black.

This Is the Room

This is the room full of doubt where I sit and write my poems. It is a room with two windows facing an open street with no clear view of the sky. It is a room with no mirrors and no pictures. It is a room full of electric light. This is where I write amongst the music books and guitar picks, amongst the power cables and the acoustic guitar. I rack my brain in this room and still I wake up in the morning, walk in circles, read Whitman aloud and wish he were my grandfather because this is the room I was born in.

The Aim Is True

In the dusk of my nightmares
I see no pale star
But a globe moon
Thin like wax paper
Floating in a great full tree
I feel it like ice
Straight down my throat
The pain of leaving
The pain of tearing
A blackbird in the sky
No sound but the ripping
Of corduroy jackets
Into the sky
Fat chunks of meat
I never knew you could be so full
Yet still break so easy

There Is No Motel Room
That Can Fit Me

3 a.m. soda machine,
Sweaty change and I can taste
The ammonia in my last cigarette.
Next door
A woman moans.
I grab some ice from the green bucket.
Place it in a thin white rag,
Smash it with the Bible.
Put the rag on my eyes.
Picture myself
On the girl
But I moan
And she works.
Tomorrow, Vegas.
Tonight, Lusk.

Well, Well, Well

Said the lightning bug
To the spider
"You bitch, you ain't my kin."

Said the spider
To the lightning bug
"I ate my children
And now I am going to do you a favor."

Said the lightning bug
To the spider
"You going to suck me dry? I fly you idiot."

Said the spider
To the lightning bug
"My web knows no bounds, no flight and no gravity
You will be my new heartbeat.
I'll sleep in your glow,
Watch you die slowly."

Said the lightning bug
To the spider
"Let me go."
Said the spider
To the lightning bug
"Hush my little 40-watt bulb, hush."

Do You Envy the Dead?

Do you envy the dead?
Do you prefer to be a corpse in the ground?
Cold and bursting at the seams of your funeral gown?
Everyone who knew you or loved you has left you
To a short dash pounded in granite.

Jesus in Mankato

My mother was in the hospital for a week.

The last of my clothes on my back

I needed to wash the rest.

So I went to the Laundromat on the corner

From the hotel where I was staying.

I used the change from the last five dollar bill to my name.

Threw everything in together.

Found a seat by the window and waited.

I was hungry but couldn't eat.

I was lost in my mind and there he came

With his sandals, brown pants and his white shirt hanging loose in the
          winter sun.

He sat across from me, picked up the paper and read in silence.

I noticed that when he turned the pages he left red bloodstains on
          the corners.

His feet were bruised but not bleeding.

I got messages on my phone, *"What's going on? How is she? What did
the doctors say? What is the diagnosis? Is she able to eat? Can she come
home? When will that be? Who is going to take her?"*

I turned it off and looked at Jesus.

But I left him there, checked on my clothes,

Put them in the dryer and sat by the window.

The snow glared at me and I stared back, blinded.

On Driving by the Wounded Knee Massacre Site Every Day to School

All the dead should
Arise and start dancing.
The dead should come
In bright clothing.
The dead should bring
Back the Ghost Dance.
The dead should sing
In high spiraling voices.

Evidence of Existence

Left behind as evidence of existence:
A coffee cup smelling of your breakfast blend
Sugar packets
Shoes worn, scuffed by travel
A jacket with the smell of perfume on the collar
Blankets and a pillow with mascara on the side
Your car with the coffee stains in the cup holder
Four boxes of Gevalia unopened
Jewelry, watches, and earrings missing their other half
Strands of hair in the comb on the dresser
Insulin needles, pill bottles both full and empty
Books read, books started, pages folded and unfinished
Papers covered in the purple ink of your cursive hand
Your last set of clothes, crumpled in your suitcase
And we three

Backseat Los Angeles

Outside, the copper light
Of refineries pump the earth.
You sit in the backseat of a car
Going 85 miles an hour
To some city on the west coast.
To sleep in a hotel with a thin mattress
But a view of the ocean.
Just to find out that yes the world is old
And yes you are young, lost
And unmemorable.

My Dog Carrying a Frozen Snake

My dog carrying a frozen snake.
The smell of dead things on the cuff
Of my funeral shirt.
Sweet vinegar, dirt on my feet.
I want to fight someone.
My bloody hands and me will walk anywhere.
There is a halo around the light pole.
My heart buried in the mud.
I dig it out, take it inside and place it
On my mother's kitchen table.
Take out the cutlery from the closet.
Use the best plate, the broken one.

July 3rd, 1983

There he goes strollin' to the river
With his fixin'-to-die rag on.

Left letters on the table typed.
Had a joint with me.
"Tell the ones who need to know," he said.

"Why the letters?" I asked.
"Just for decoration," he answered.

He left me high as a kite.
My string caught in the rosebush.

The Graveyard the Poems Not Written

The graveyard
The poems not written
I take the black mare
As a sign
It's ok to mourn
I take the glowing river
As a sign
It's ok to feel
The headless snake still has heart
A silent boat
On an ancient tributary
That's where I go

The Reality of Limitation

Boiling potatoes in the dark
An urge to grab one so I do
The fire waves under the pot
The only light a blue light
Like a flag in summer
My hand burns, the potato smokes
I crush it through my fingers boiling white
My hand blisters
The only light in the room a blue flag in summer
The only sound in the room me crying at the sink

A Fog over the Hills

A fog over the hills
Blacked out the lights of my neighbors
A globe of loneliness
And my mother is in the ground
And my brother is out somewhere
There are sounds coming from the kitchen
Cooking sounds
I decide to stand outside
With the lights off and listen

After

I drive home in the December dark
A neverending landscape of black and white hills
Pockets, twists, ice and concrete
Alone for an hour and a half
Coming up to the hill near the house
Three doe prance over the road
Children without a mother

II.

In the Department Store above the World

In the department store above the world/
I plot my war/
Gather my Coke bottle bombs/
Steak knife rifles/
Fashion my body in warrior paint/
Have words with my ancestors in the spoon/
Exit—
Drop to the grass—
Eat the dirt—

Time\
Composed\
Golden pocket watch\

Snakeskin sex/
Root beer cream caves/
A blue flame/ sparking like a wildflower/
Keep calling me so I can find you/
My wife/ the river has gone dry/
I can't dip—
My finger in her—
Anymore—

Hands\
Blood broken\
Spread the meat\

In a field/
In a snowstorm/
Arms aloft/
My body/ blossomed with bruises/
The sting of galaxies/ cut my thin frame/
Enter Indio god—
Break me like a father—
The flowers of victory—

Spiral staircase\
Tracing\
DNA brain grains\

From the leaf notebook/
A sentiment/
As bright as a jar/ broken into pieces/
A rainbow specter/
Dusty muscle/
I am not you—you are not me—but those birds—
Those sparrows know us—

The egg\

Undone\

If I could do anything I would bring
You back, lay you down on your bed
And open the window

The Broken Rhyme of the Ancient Traveler

"Purple thistles,
White lilies
And the golden
Birds of spring,
Nothing can kill
The mood I'm in

Except maybe
An owl with big
Bright eyes and
Blood stained wings.

Amber wheat,
Yellow sunflowers
And the blue
Snakes of spring,
Nothing can kill
The state I'm in

Except maybe
A firefly trailing
Its glowing insides
On the air, spelling
Beware."

What Nightmares Will Come

I was singing at my brother's funeral.

The chairs were in a straight line.

His casket was closed.

Just the day before he was talking to me.

We were at our mother's house cooking eggs, scrambled.

I should have known.

His shirt was too bright.

But he smiled and was happy.

We were eating eggs and he said, "I died outside.

You have to find my body."

So I told him I would.

"But stay here with mom." I said,

"Give her some comfort."

I gave him one last hug and went outside.

I found him in a field.

We buried him underneath a pale dawn sky

Over and over again.

White Suit, White Coffin

Thought he was made of plastic.
White suit and rhinestones,
White coffin.

Thought it was a story adults told,
Semi-truck suction,
Stay off the road.

Thought he was just sleeping in there.
No marks, no cuts, no bruises
Just sleeping.

Even Jesus had blood on his feet and hands.
A spear in his side left a scar.
I saw it, marked and traced it, there it was.

This boy, nothing.

Just white suit and white coffin.

Wokiksuye

I cross a small bridge into St. Paul. I feel the troubled waters. I think of my grandfather's people, the Dakota. I think of how they lived by the water, how they made fire by the water. I think of how my people were taken to Fort Snelling Prison. I think of Many Lightnings and his sons, my family, every time I see the "Historic Site" sign coming into St. Paul. I think of how the 38 sang their prayer and death songs. I think of how my family watched their people hang all together.

I try to *see* this but the red and green lights distract me. I try to *hear* them but the tires screeching and the horns honking distract me. All I have are signs, another "Historic Site Fort Snelling" ahead. All I have is dirty water under a bridge. I don't have their voices. I don't have their words. So I drive into St. Paul, park my car and walk amongst the cold leaves to my apartment building. I manage only a small token of smoke and silence.

Lucky,

My brother was able
To drive home through
The badlands at 4 a.m.
His eyes hadn't swollen
Shut. His face covered
By a blue rag, from nose
To neck, to hide the blood,
Cuts and swelling.
He told me how he woke
Up on a carpet in a dark
Room and how he found
A man at a car wash
Willing to give him a ride
Back to his truck in some
Dark apartment parking lot.
In the end he laughed
With all his teeth.
The moon was my compass,
He said.
I knew where to go.

The Sad Punk's Winter in Youth

I lived during
The coldest winter
Months,
With no hot food or car,
High as a kite,
Warm from alcohol.

I remember the blanket
Of white
Taking my breath away.

We walked,
My cousin and I,
Down an icy black road.

Heat coming from our bellies
A mixture of tequila
And sticky smokes.
We had to walk
6 miles in the cold
To watch some Chinese films.

The Sad True Tales of J. Strait:
In Which There Is Contemplation

I
Satan is bright
And blooming
On the highway
Into my heart.
I'm not an old blues man
But I understand
That rank dark of the bedroom
And the bright death of a Sunday morning.
I bathe in the glory of the word.
I fear it.
Nothing moves me
But the melody of cat gut.
Praise be to the son and the father,
That bastard absent.
Amen.

II
Lost my place, my fire
To a whore in a blue room.
While she took it from me
I turned my head and watched

The moon turn golden.
On the dirty bed she groaned
But I was left to wonder,
Why so blue?
Why not golden?

III
He likes to hit them.
My mother—
That was all she knew.
He tried to teach me
But I was strange.
I wanted to give them
Roses not bruises, not
Cuts and lashes.
My father said, you are
Strange.
But still I gave
My mother roses.

IV
I drink diesel
Before I hitch
Eat a bologna sandwich
Before I hitch
Cut my left arm

Before I hitch
Make sure I have weed
Before I hitch
Say a prayer to Orion
Before I hitch
Call on all my ghosts
Before I hitch
Light the match
Before I hitch

V
Backseats are perfect.
I can watch the world,
Be content in its passing.
I can put both of my hands
Out of the window
Spread my fingers,
Become a bird.

VI
Bluebird,
Whisper for me.
Leave a message with my mother.
Tell her I'm sorry.
Tell her I didn't try.
But let her know I've got her rosary

In my breast pocket,
The only thing worth saving
On me.
Tell mother I love her.
I love her only.

VII
To the wild coyotes of Augusta:
Don't take my blood away.
Leave me my bones.
Leave the energy of your eyes,
The heat of your breath.
Take away that smell.
Bring back the glory of sunflowers and deep black earth.

VIII
This Arizona smoke is soft.
I buy an ounce with the money in my left shoe,
Retreat to the desert
By way of the all-night diner,
Alone and curious.
I get lost in the red rocks find a cove of earth
And build a fire.
Dig a grave for my son.
Make a table for my father.
Wait for the snakes

To nip my knees,
Tear into my Achilles tendon,
Make me cry.

IX

That Irish whiskey has left me lonely.
To live out the remaining years on my toilet,
My guts on fire and crackling to burst.
It was good times though, Pittsburgh oil
And coal dust. A warm Nordic goddess
And lust. A good card game.
Got me some money left in pocket.
Remember her name.
I must remember her name.

X

Got into a fight
With a fat trucker from Paw Paw
By way of West Virginia.
He didn't like my laugh.
Couldn't help it I said.
Paw Paw. Pretty soon
We were under the half-moon night.
Boy he hit my head something fierce,
Ham-hand slaps, tree-trunk whacks.
Left me on the dirt laughing through my bloody

Mouth.
I had to wash my brain in the sink
Full of dirt. It smelled of nachos.
I coated it with a baby goose egg
And let it dry
While I sat on the floor, lotus style, naked
With a warm Pabst in my hand.

XI
I like diner food
Nice and greasy
I like diner tables
Sticky in places
I like diner chairs
Old and creaky
I like diner views
Flat landscape poetry
I like diner lighting
Bright and shiny
I like diner women
They always smile
I want to die in a diner
In some random act of violence
I want that man, with the limp,
Coming in to do it
I am looking right at him

Come on man kill me
Right here, right now
I don't want to go to Vegas
Put me out of my misery

XII
She keeps yelling at me
Louder and louder
I feel nothing
I can't read her face
All red and wet
All I see is her mouth
And as she stands in the doorway
Blocking me
All I can think is
I want to hit her but I'm not my father
So keep yelling
I'm gonna count the kitchen tiles

XIII
The moon
Fat and golden
Hanging in the atmosphere
Licking the tops of the hills
All around me
Hello moon

Just you and me tonight
How are you?
Me you ask?
Just resting with my back on the earth
Counting stars
Had to stop at ten
Made me sad if I am honest
All that light
So far away
I like lying on the earth
Not in it
Not yet

XIV
Planes trick me at night
I think they are sliding stars
Off to some planetary playground
In the wake of the crescent moon
I long for a fishing pole
I blame my mother
She made me love things like the moon

XV
Drunk and hungry
Grab a bag of chips from the trash
There's a broken bottle

On the street
Some beer left in it
The sun gives it color
I'm trying
But trying is hard
Especially when my stomach is empty
My lighter doesn't work
And I got one cigarette left
I'm trying
To keep myself
From the razorblade
Lord, my name is J_____
And I am your bastard son

XVI
I've got nothing left in me but unleaded gasoline
And a sliver of water near my clavicle
I sniff it to keep me human

There is just this road
This black road where the lines are golden
And the grass is silver

Somewhere down this road a crow calls me
By my name, calling in my mother's voice
Ready to slap me for making mistakes

XVII

No matter where I am
When I wake I pray
Not to Jesus, the fool,
But to the emperor moth
I pray to its multicolored corpse
Its death so I could dream
I pray and give it thanks
Make like a bandit
Before the cavalry comes
And then take a few breaths
Ready for the road ahead

III.

The Pale Trumpet Sings the Blues

In a dream my grandfather handed it to me.
In a dream he had both eyes and walked again.
The trumpet pale and brittle in his hands.

In the basement of his house we sat
On a bench. In his hands the trumpet sang.

The Suicide Girl in Marfa, Texas

Dying to the music of Son House.
She missed the last truck out of town.
No one was home to meet her anyway.
All gone to Mexico in the backseat of cars.
She spent the night underneath Christmas lights
Outside a white stucco Laundromat.
The suicide girl had decided
To get a beer, mix it with her pills
And walk over to the train tracks.
Wait
For a lonesome whistle
To slide over her body.

The Cool Calm Love of a Nightmare

I could go for some
Red-blooded
Bluegrass murder.

Tales of beheadings
And dirty dinner
Deals.

All in the
Holy name of
A bloody Christ.

Tall tales
Of sons and
Daughters

In love with one
Another
Plotting suicide

With wood violets
In their hair
And moonshine

On their incestuous
Tongues so velvet
Wet.

I could use
Some devil-may-care
Violin solos.

Thick, heavy
Rusted horsehair strings
Plucked, fucked and

Pulled to silver
Blue perfection
In the dark

Of the halls of a
Faded hand-built
Church.

Led by the teachings
Of a man
Touched by

The Lamb of God
In the form

Of an archangel.

Till the three chords strike
And we all
Fall down.

They Say the Past Comes Trembling

I place the bones on the table.
Gather the sinew string and begin the work.
I take the door off the hinges
And throw the screws into a bottle of vodka.
The wind brings ash and smoke.
By the time I have finished
My eyes begin tearing.
Between two vases of bright yellow tulips
The bones catch the light
And cast the reason on me.

Grasp the World in an Embrace and Fall Back

The landscape under the moon,
The road a glow rug of death.
Right now this is the hour of my soul.
I spread my arms wide, grasp the world in an embrace and fall back.

A Poet of Bright Feathers

I am ready for love / Too many funerals make my hands hurt / I
have used up my pennies for their eyes / The animals left / The birds
attacked me / I was too bright for them / They pecked my ribs / Tore
into my legs / And left me at the bottom of a small tree / Where I have
chosen to recite the words of Blake / I understand his grief / Here I lie
/ A broken bright mess /

The Quiet Room

Sea salt and vinegar poured on the table
Bring the body here
Two men carry the boy across the threshold and place him gently
Down on the dark wood
Shut the door and leave us
In the silence of the room occupied by two one breathes
Deep into the bones and tries to remember the words
But first the dark
The woman closes the windows and covers them with sheets
Dark has become a physical space
That bounces when she walks through it
Finding the body
She places her fingers in his cold mouth

It Feels Like Love

A red turtle
Somewhere in the chest there is an egg
Pink as frost in the sunset
Knife black
Cut through shell
Thick strings of blood and vein and life itself
I reach in
I hear you mother
Collapse lung
Full-bodied aneurysm
I float in the blue world
I lack nothing

Unfaithful Servant

I'm an unfaithful servant
I am an unholy ghost
Walking barefoot
On the salted ice street
Behold the ego and the ax
I grab both and aim for the oak
I've never done well on land
I hide my boots in the river
I place worms in my hair
I decide when and where we cut each other
Before this world ends
Let's get drunk on homemade wine
Let's touch each other like children
Marvel at this and that
In my left hand a bottle of ink
To drink and drink
To swallow and spit and then sleep
Underneath you

Peace and Love

Peace and love is lying in a bathroom
Downtown near the train station
Peace and love is ready to take a deep dive
Inside the cracks of the gay bar
Peace and love is breaking her hands on the mirrors
Collecting the shards
Peace and love walks out the door and into the warm city night
Sliding like a ghost between moving bodies
Peace and love stands under a neon sign reading CHECKS CASHED HERE
Listening to the hum of gas and electricity
Peace and love reaches in her pockets
She throws a handful of broken mirror into the air

Van Gogh Cared Too Much

Van Gogh cared too much
Didn't have the strength to realize
That really it doesn't matter
Everyone comes to it after you've left the room
He did see the fire first
Sat by it
Ran his fingers through the soft flame
Talked with it and was burned
He waited for company
He smoked and drank coffee
And he waited for someone to come see
By then
The bloom set in
Creeping like oil into the sides of his skull
No one ever came to visit
To say a word
To shake his hand
So into the fields he went

I've Seen It Come Alive

I saw him fly into the air
When he came down
There was nothing to cradle him except the ground

I hit my brakes
I stayed in the car waiting for someone to come

An hour passed
A hand grabbed my car hood
He stood up pale as snow
And walked toward the cream-colored badlands

I watched him
The sky was fat with pink clouds
There was no wind though
Just stillness

He stopped in the middle of the field before the badlands
I've never heard a scream so beautiful
It ripped my heart out
And ate of it

The Warriors of the Painted Horse

The warriors of the painted horse
Had a tradition
Kill a badger and pour its blood
Into a hole in the ground
One by one they looked inside
If they saw themselves old
They would live
If they saw themselves as they were
They would die
And still they left
Ready to battle
Sticking their flags into the earth

In My Arm a Shipwreck

In my arm
    A shipwreck
        Freezing
I've decided to do the laundry
    At the 22 hour place
    It's 3:00 a.m.
I've decided to use the good detergent
    Saved enough quarters
One had Panama on the back
Found a seat near the cold black windows
    On the TV above a game show
        Millions of dollars and I can't get a cup of coffee
A kid, 4 or so, plays a shooter game
    His shirt bright green, it blinds me
        I stare so long
            The dad gives me a look
My arm
    Stings like death
        I pull out my Bible
            Of blank pages
I've decided to remake myself
I have a home with a bed
I have a dog and a yard

I have a car that gets me where I need to go
  Buzz Buzz my clothes are done
    Spinning like a carousel
      In my hands I take unto them and place them into the dryer
Slam the last of what I call funds into the clicking machine
  A woman on TV has won millions
    The boy in green is eating a candy bar
I rest a while between a dryer and the wall
    Close my eyes and place my head on the gentle warm hum of energy
In my arm
    Icicles
I recall reading about a man who cut into his own shoulder, scooped out
      the cancer with a spoon
Purple balloons of sickness
In my dream a man, a field and a storm
    I race to the one star I can see and
      I am on a shore filled with purple fish, flopping for air
A ship glowing in the water
    Neon green
Pulsating brighter and darker, brighter and darker
A hand on my arm
I wake up and see the world and see the boy in front of me with his
      stained face
It's 3:45 a.m.
I have traveled the world and back

Paradise Lost

I wonder if paradise lies with her eyes open
And her arms spread out like wings
Warm from the sun.

I wonder if she waits for someone
To come and wet her hands with
Water from the ocean.

I wonder if she has decided to wait
Until the moon is full and the tides
Turn pale.

The final stroll down her beach made soft and warm.

The final stroll across smooth rocks with veins of pearl.

I wonder if she will decide that this is the moment,

To let herself down in warm water
Full and pregnant with lustrous fish.

Lit and Motionless

I lie underneath
A beast of pine.
Stare for a star so bright it crawls to me.
I find the moon
A sliver of thumbnail pink.
Behind me a wolf.
To the left a snake.
In front a white bull, horns bleeding.
Am I ready to die?
Not yet little star, little prince of moonbeam.
Not yet.

Moon Psalm

When the children started crying
I felt bad so I threw her
Into the dark.

Prayers with
My Little Plastic Jesus

My little plastic Jesus sits on my dashboard.
My little plastic Jesus has dominion over the dashboard.
My little plastic Jesus blesses the windshield.
My little plastic Jesus blesses the steering wheel
And together we pray
Bless this car, bless its wheels,
Bless its almighty engine, may we
Get there and may we get back.
Amen.

My little plastic Jesus has a pink halo that warms me at night.
My little plastic Jesus asks only for a kiss on his small brown feet.

The Prayer

For the full moon that forced my hands
I say I love you for it.
For the planets that die before I wake
I say forgive me for it.
For the child unborn inside my body
I say you'll thank me for it.

The Mechanics of My Heart

Find a corner shop.
Cigarettes and a Coke
12 bucks.
Light up in the alley.
Remember you can't smoke anywhere anymore.
Walk until I see water.
Listen to the water carry boats and people.
Remember Whitman
And his poem about the ferry.
I want to ride it.
Try and be open with my heart.
Try to recall I am human
And so are you.
And when we all die, and we will, we shall sleep in God's green beard
       together.

I'm Thankful for the Blues

I'm thankful for the blues
The fogged windows of cars
The muted city lights
The static of small radio stations
The violin, mandolin, heartbeat of song

I'm thankful for neon lights
The painted signs in canary yellow
The open doors of small town bars
The rusted trucks parked in empty lots
The tumbling heat of desert winds

I'm thankful for the ache of cold nights
The motels of one light bulb, green bed sheets
The all-night diners of hot coffee
The four-wheeled angel
The passenger side, the open window

The population 15, the name Wisdom

Late Night Driving

I like driving at night on the reservation.
Blanketed by the dark
It looks like it can sleep through the night.
But one must be ready.
Anything and everything lives.
The road is a map known only in the wrists.
One second it's clear yellow and white lines
Then there is a two-foot-tall fat porcupine
Just sitting in the middle of the road, then
There are two men staggering the final mile toward
Home, swaying on the nonexistent breeze.
You learn what it means to be the lone car, the
Only person at that moment blasting the radio
Loud, you are aware of what it means to be the lone
Sound amongst the dead, and just when you think
It can't get dark enough there in the east the sky sparks
Red lightning.

A Poor Funeral, a Good Meal, Father

I had dug a small grave. Not
Deep but underneath the tree
The dirt was soft. I lay him
Inside, his fifty-cent piece on his
Chest along with David Copperfield.
I had nothing to say except,
Say hello to all the wives for me.
Say hello to my little brothers and sisters.
I covered him with dirt. Went inside. Made
Myself steak with green onions. Drank
The rest of his beer and whiskey. Played
My best song on the old piano.
Minor chords only.

To the Wolves of Chernobyl

We won't bother you anymore.
After we tried to force you over the ice river
You tore my brother's arms off but we don't blame you.
We know how it is to be taken from home
To some gleaming city in the dark
Where they speak in another tongue and eat strange food.
We know what it is to keep your pups where their ancestors lived.
My brother thanks you
For leaving his bones at the door.

Moments Have You

We swam in silence,
My brother and I,
The green glass water
Trembling around us.
In that moment I was God
And would always be
For there is none but me
When the times are rough
And when people die.
The green glass held us,
Let us float awhile
And then it broke.
We had enough, didn't want
To be cut anymore than we
Already were.
We made shore
And drove home
With windows down,
A fat joint between us, poetry.

To Return as a Vessel

When I come back I'll be a boat,
Weather beaten.
My body will be worthy.

In the day I will carry you
Out into the water,
Listen as you sing in any language.

In the night,
I will take you to a soft spot,
Cradle you
Underneath the night sky.

I'll be the earth for you in the dark.

My Childhood House

My childhood house has
Four wheels, windshield cracked and torn warm leather seats.
Its voice is a low moan, its song a lullaby
Cradling me at night, letting me sleep with the windows open.
Its kindness in the summertime,
Warm hood, reflection eye, sky spreading forever.
Lying in the backseat, the flights of treetops and
The stars still, humming.

Author Acknowledgments

It's a small book but it took work to make it a book. My thanks go out to Jim Moore, Deborah Keenan, Patricia Kirkpatrick, Gretchen Marquette and Caitlin Bailey. I would also like to acknowledge my brothers Lloyd and Louis for being my brothers, my family.

This book is dedicated to the memory and the life of my mother.

Tavern Books

Tavern Books is a not-for-profit poetry publisher that exists to print, promote, and preserve works of literary vision, to foster a climate of cultural preservation, and to disseminate books in a way that benefits the reading public.

We publish books in translation from the world's finest poets, champion new works by innovative writers, and revive out-of-print classics. We keep our titles in print, honoring the cultural contract between publisher and author, as well as between publisher and public. Our catalog, known as The Living Library, sustains the visions of our authors, ensuring their voices remain alive in the social and artistic discourse of our modern era.

About the Wrolstad Series

To honor the life and work of Greta Wrolstad (1981-2005), author of *Night is Simply a Shadow* (2013) and *Notes on Sea & Shore* (2010), Tavern Books invites submissions of new poetry collections through the Wrolstad Contemporary Poetry Series during an annual reading period.

This series exists to champion exceptional literary works from young women poets through book publication in The Living Library, the Tavern Books catalog of innovative poets ranging from first-time authors and neglected masters to Pulitzer Prize winners and Nobel Laureates. The Wrolstad Contemporary Poetry Series is open to any woman aged 40 years or younger who is a US citizen, a legal resident of the U.S., or has DACA, TPS, or LPS status, regardless of publication history.

For more information visit: www.tavernbooks.org/wrolstad-ser/

Subscriptions

Become a subscriber and receive the next six Tavern Books titles at a substantial discount, delivered to your door. Paperback and hardcover subscriptions available.

For details visit www.tavernbooks.org or write to us at:

Tavern Books
at Union Station
800 NW 6th Avenue #255
Portland, Oregon 97209

The Living Library

Killing Floor by Ai
with an introduction by Major Jackson

Arthur's Talk with the Eagle by Anonymous,
translated from the Welsh by Gwyneth Lewis

Ashulia by Zubair Ahmed

The Blind Plain by Igor Barreto,
translated from the Spanish by Rowena Hill

Breckinridge County Suite by Joe Bolton

My People & Other Poems by Wojciech Bonowicz,
translated from the Polish by Piotr Florczyk

Who Lives by Elisabeth Borchers,
translated from the German by Caroline Wilcox Reul

Buson: Haiku by Yosa Buson,
translated from the Japanese by Franz Wright

Poems 1904 by C.P. Cavafy,
translated from the Greek by Paul Merchant

Evidence of What Is Said by Ann Charters and Charles Olson

In the Shadow Country by Elena Cisneros

Who Whispered Near Me by Killarney Clary

The End of Space by Albert Goldbarth

Six-Minute Poems: The Last Poems
by George Hitchcock

The Wounded Alphabet: Collected Poems
by George Hitchcock

Hitchcock on Trial
by George Hitchcock

At the Devil's Banquets by Anise Koltz,
translated from the French by John F. Deane

My Blue Piano by Else Lasker-Schüler,
translated from the German by Eavan Boland

What Have I to Say to You by Megan Levad

Why We Live in the Dark Ages by Megan Levad

Archeology by Adrian C. Louis

Fire Water World & Among the Dog Eaters
by Adrian C. Louis

Emergency Brake by Ruth Madievsky

Under an Arkansas Sky by Jo McDougall

The Undiscovered Room by Jo McDougall

Ocean by Joseph Millar

Petra by Amjad Nasser,
translated from the Arabic by Fady Joudah

The Fire's Journey: Part I by Eunice Odio,
translated from the Spanish by Keith Ekiss
with Sonia P. Ticas and Mauricio Espinoza

The Fire's Journey: Part II by Eunice Odio,
translated from the Spanish by Keith Ekiss
with Sonia P. Ticas and Mauricio Espinoza

The Fire's Journey: Part III by Eunice Odio,
translated from the Spanish by Keith Ekiss
with Sonia P. Ticas and Mauricio Espinoza

*The Fire's Journey: Part IV by Eunice Odio,
translated from the Spanish by Keith Ekiss
with Sonia P. Ticas and Mauricio Espinoza

Full Body Pleasure Suit by Elsbeth Pancrazi

Duino Elegies by Rainer Maria Rilke,
translated from the German by Gary Miranda

Twelve Poems About Cavafy by Yannis Ritsos,
translated from the Greek by Paul Merchant

Monochords by Yannis Ritsos,
translated from the Greek by Paul Merchant

Glowing Enigmas by Nelly Sachs,
translated from the German by Michael Hamburger

Prodigy by Charles Simic,
drawings by Charles Seluzicki

Night of Shooting Stars by Leonardo Sinisgalli,
translated from the Italian by W. S. Di Piero

Skin by Tone Škrjanec,
translated from the Slovene by Matthew Rohrer and Ana Pepelnik

We Women by Edith Södergran,
translated from the Swedish by Samuel Charters

Winterward by William Stafford

Building the Barricade by Anna Świrszczyńska,
translated from the Polish by Piotr Florczyk,
with an introduction by Eavan Boland

Baltics by Tomas Tranströmer,
with photographs by Ann Charters,
translated from the Swedish by Samuel Charters

For the Living and the Dead by Tomas Tranströmer,
translated from the Swedish by John F. Deane

Prison: Nine Haiku from Hällby Youth Prison by Tomas Tranströmer,
translated from the Swedish by Malena Mörling

Tomas Tranströmer's First Poems & Notes from the Land of Lap Fever
by Tomas Tranströmer and Jonas Ellerström,
translated from the Swedish by Malena Mörling

Collected Translations by David Wevill

Casual Ties by David Wevill

Where the Arrow Falls by David Wevill

A Christ of the Ice-Floes by David Wevill

Night Is Simply a Shadow by Greta Wrolstad

Notes on Sea & Shore by Greta Wrolstad

The Countries We Live In by Natan Zach,
translated from the Hebrew by Peter Everwine

*forthcoming

Tavern Books is funded, in part, by the generosity of philanthropic organizations, public and private institutions, and individual donors.

By supporting Tavern Books and its mission, you enable us to publish the most exciting poets from around the world. To learn more about underwriting Tavern Books titles, please contact us by e-mail: info@tavernbooks.org.

MAJOR FUNDING HAS BEEN PROVIDED BY

THE LIBRA FOUNDATION   **Lannan**

OREGON ARTS
COMMISSION

ADDITIONAL FUNDING PROVIDED BY

Dean & Karen Garyet
Bill & Leah Stenson
Mark Swartz & Jennifer Jones
Mary Ann Ryan
Wendy Willis & David Biespiel
Ron & Kathy Wrolstad

Colophon

This book was designed and typeset by Eldon Potter at Bryan Potter Design, Portland, Oregon. Text is set in Garamond, an old-style serif typeface named for the punch-cutter Claude Garamond (c. 1480-1561). Display font is Eczar: designed by Vaibhav Singh, published by Rosetta; paid for and distributed by Google. *In the Shadow Country* appears in both paperback and cloth-covered editions. Printed on archival-quality paper by McNaughton & Gunn, Inc.